Note: *This is NOT a legal document and does not replace any wills or other documentation mentioned herein.*

Ella Dawn Creations

Copyright protected. All rights reserved.
Electronic or printed reproduction is prohibited without written consent from the author.

AFTER DEATH JOURNAL

WRITTEN BY

_____

TO THOSE WHO READ THIS JOURNAL

TO THOSE WHO READ THIS JOURNAL

TO THOSE WHO READ THIS JOURNAL

TO THOSE WHO READ THIS JOURNAL

PERSONAL INFORMATION

PERSONAL INFORMATION

FULL LEGAL NAME

MAIDEN SURNAME

KNOWN TO MOST AS

NICKNAMES

BIRTH DATE

PLACE OF BIRTH

PERSONAL IDENTIFICATION NUMBERS

ID NUMBER	
WHERE TO FIND IT	

TAX NUMBER	
WHERE TO FIND IT	

PASSPORT NUMBER	
WHERE TO FIND IT	

PERSONAL INFORMATION

QUALIFICATIONS

MY RELIGION AND INVOLVEMENT

OTHER

PERSONAL INFORMATION

(Additional space has been provided so that you can keep this information up to date)

POSTAL ADDRESS	P.O. BOX KEY IS LOCATED

DATES AT THIS ADDRESS: FROM _____ TO _____

POSTAL ADDRESS	P.O. BOX KEY IS LOCATED

DATES AT THIS ADDRESS: FROM _____ TO _____

POSTAL ADDRESS	P.O. BOX KEY IS LOCATED

DATES AT THIS ADDRESS: FROM _____ TO _____

POSTAL ADDRESS	P.O. BOX KEY IS LOCATED

DATES AT THIS ADDRESS: FROM _____ TO _____

PERSONAL INFORMATION

(Additional space has been provided so that you can keep this information up to date)

PHYSICAL ADDRESS

DATES AT THIS ADDRESS: FROM _____ TO _____

PHYSICAL ADDRESS

DATES AT THIS ADDRESS: FROM _____ TO _____

PHYSICAL ADDRESS

DATES AT THIS ADDRESS: FROM _____ TO _____

PHYSICAL ADDRESS

DATES AT THIS ADDRESS: FROM _____ TO _____

PERSONAL INFORMATION

TELEPHONE NUMBER	
MOBILE NUMBER	PROVIDER
OTHER CONTACT NUMBERS	

EMAIL ADDRESS	ACCESS VIA	PASSWORD

NOTES

MY FAMILY

A COPY OF MY FAMILY TREE IS LOCATED

MY PARENTS		
MOTHER	BORN	DIED
FATHER	BORN	DIED
WHERE MARRIED	DATE	DIVORCED
MORE ABOUT MY PARENTS		

MY SPOUSE/S			
NAME		BORN	DIED
WHERE WE WERE MARRIED		DATE	DIVORCED
NAME		BORN	DIED
WHERE WE WERE MARRIED		DATE	DIVORCED
NAME		BORN	DIED
WHERE WE WERE MARRIED		DATE	DIVORCED

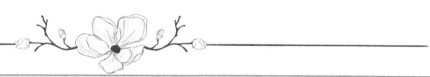

MY CHILDREN		
NAME		BORN
SCHOOL		
ALLERGIES & MEDICATIONS	DOCTOR	DR TEL
OTHER		
NAME		BORN
SCHOOL		
ALLERGIES & MEDICATIONS	DOCTOR	DR TEL
OTHER		
NAME		BORN
SCHOOL		
ALLERGIES & MEDICATIONS	DOCTOR	DR TEL
OTHER		
NAME		BORN
SCHOOL		
ALLERGIES & MEDICATIONS	DOCTOR	DR TEL
OTHER		

MY CHILDREN

NAME		BORN	
SCHOOL			
ALLERGIES & MEDICATIONS	DOCTOR		DR TEL
OTHER			

NAME		BORN	
SCHOOL			
ALLERGIES & MEDICATIONS	DOCTOR		DR TEL
OTHER			

NAME		BORN	
SCHOOL			
ALLERGIES & MEDICATIONS	DOCTOR		DR TEL
OTHER			

NAME		BORN	
SCHOOL			
ALLERGIES & MEDICATIONS	DOCTOR		DR TEL
OTHER			

MY GRANDCHILDREN	
NAME	BORN
PARENTS	
NAME	BORN
PARENTS	
NAME	BORN
PARENTS	
NAME	BORN
PARENTS	
NAME	BORN
PARENTS	
NAME	BORN
PARENTS	
NAME	BORN
PARENTS	
NAME	BORN
PARENTS	
NAME	BORN
PARENTS	

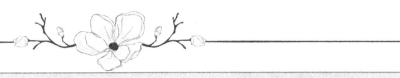

MY GRANDCHILDREN	
NAME	BORN
PARENTS	
NAME	BORN
PARENTS	
NAME	BORN
PARENTS	
NAME	BORN
PARENTS	
NAME	BORN
PARENTS	
NAME	BORN
PARENTS	
NAME	BORN
PARENTS	
NAME	BORN
PARENTS	
NAME	BORN
PARENTS	

MY PETS

VET	VET TEL

PET CARE ARRANGEMENTS ON MY PASSING

MY PETS

NAME	BREED

SPECIAL INSTRUCTIONS

NAME	BREED

SPECIAL INSTRUCTIONS

NAME	BREED

SPECIAL INSTRUCTIONS

NAME	BREED

SPECIAL INSTRUCTIONS

MY PETS

NAME	BREED
SPECIAL INSTRUCTIONS	

NAME	BREED
SPECIAL INSTRUCTIONS	

NAME	BREED
SPECIAL INSTRUCTIONS	

NAME	BREED
SPECIAL INSTRUCTIONS	

NOTES

NOTES

MEDICAL INFORMATION

MEDICAL INFORMATION

MEDICAL AID	POLICY NUMBER
CONTACT NO	
NOTES	

IN THE EVENT THAT I BECOME INCAPACITATED

MY BLOOD TYPE	
HOSPITAL OF CHOICE	CONTACT
MY NOMINATED HEALTH CARE POWER OF ATTORNEY IS	CONTACT
THE HEALTH CARE POWER OF ATTORNEY DOCUMENT IS LOCATED	
MY LIVING WILL CAN BE FOUND	
MY DO NOT RESUSCITATE DOCUMENT CAN BE FOUND	
MY ORGAN DONOR DOCUMENT CAN BE FOUND	

MY DOCTORS

GP NAME	CONTACT NUMBER
NOTES	

SPECIALIST NAME	CONTACT NUMBER
TYPE OF SPECIALIST	
NOTES	

SPECIALIST NAME	CONTACT NUMBER
TYPE OF SPECIALIST	
NOTES	

SPECIALIST NAME	CONTACT NUMBER
TYPE OF SPECIALIST	
NOTES	

MY MEDICAL HISTORY

CONDITION	WHEN DIAGNOSED	TREATMENT

MY MEDICAL HISTORY

CONDITION	WHEN DIAGNOSED	TREATMENT

FAMILY MEDICAL HISTORY

ON MY MOTHER'S SIDE	ON MY FATHER'S SIDE
MY MOTHER DIED OF	MY FATHER DIED OF

MY CHILDREN'S MEDICAL HISTORY

CHILD'S NAME	CONDITION	WHEN DIAGNOSED	TREATMENT

NOTES

NOTES

FUNERAL ARRANGEMENTS

PLANNING MY FUNERAL

I HAVE A FUNERAL POLICY WITH		
POLICY NUMBER	AMOUNT	CONTACT

OTHER POLICIES TO COVER MY FUNERAL			
POLICY WITH	AMOUNT	CONTACT	NOTES

MY PREFERRED FUNERAL HOME IS	
I WOULD LIKE TO BE	
☐ **BURIED** AT THIS CEMETERY	☐ **CREMATED** AND MY ASHES DISPOSED OF HERE
NOTES FOR GRAVESTONE	

PLANNING MY FUNERAL

SPECIAL NOTES FOR THE DAY
(E.G. WHO I WOULD LIKE TO LEAD THE SERVICE, MUSIC OR HYMNS I LIKE, SPECIAL REQUESTS)

PLANNING MY FUNERAL

SPECIAL NOTES FOR THE DAY
(E.G. WHO I WOULD LIKE TO LEAD THE SERVICE, MUSIC OR HYMNS I LIKE, SPECIAL REQUESTS)

PLANNING MY FUNERAL

SPECIAL NOTES FOR THE DAY
(E.G. WHO I WOULD LIKE TO LEAD THE SERVICE, MUSIC OR HYMNS I LIKE, SPECIAL REQUESTS)

CONTACT INFORMATION

IMPORTANT CONTACTS

WHO	NAME	NUMBER / EMAIL	NOTE
PASTOR / SPIRITUAL LEADER			
ATTORNEY			
BANK			
DOCTOR			
EMPLOYER			
FUNERAL HOME			
FUNERAL POLICY			
EXECUTOR			

FAMILY MEMBERS

NAME	NUMBER / EMAIL	NOTE

FAMILY MEMBERS

NAME	NUMBER / EMAIL	NOTE

 # FAMILY MEMBERS

NAME	NUMBER / EMAIL	NOTE

FRIENDS

NAME	NUMBER / EMAIL	NOTE

FRIENDS

NAME	NUMBER / EMAIL	NOTE

FRIENDS

NAME	NUMBER / EMAIL	NOTE

ASSOCIATES, COLLEAGUES & ACQUAINTANCES

WHO	NAME	NUMBER / EMAIL	NOTE

ASSOCIATES, COLLEAGUES & ACQUAINTANCES

WHO	NAME	NUMBER / EMAIL	NOTE

ASSOCIATES, COLLEAGUES & ACQUAINTANCES

WHO	NAME	NUMBER / EMAIL	NOTE

DOCUMENTS

 # IMPORTANT DOCUMENTS

WHAT	WHERE TO FIND IT	NOTE
LAST WILL & TESTAMENT		
ID DOCUMENT		
PASSPORT		
BIRTH CERTIFICATE		
MARRIAGE CERTIFICATE		
MEDICAL INSURANCE		
TAX DOCUMENTS		
DRIVER'S LICENSE		
CHILDREN'S BIRTH CERTIFICATES		
LIFE POLICY 1:		
LIFE POLICY 2:		
LIFE POLICY 3:		
FUNERAL POLICY 1:		
FUNERAL POLICY 2:		
SHORT TERM POLICY 1:		
SHORT TERM POLICY 2:		

 # IMPORTANT DOCUMENTS

WHAT	WHERE TO FIND IT	NOTE
HOME OWNER'S POLICY:		
DEEDS TO PROPERTY 1:		
DEEDS TO PROPERTY 2:		
DEEDS TO PROPERTY 3:		
BANK CARD 1:		
BANK CARD 2:		
BANK CARD 3:		
WEBSITE / SOCIAL MEDIA ACCESS & PASSWORDS		
PET RECORDS		
PHOTO ALBUMS – PRINTED		
PHOTO ALBUMS - DIGITAL		
FAREWELL LETTERS TO LOVED ONES		

 # IMPORTANT DOCUMENTS

WHAT	WHERE TO FIND IT	NOTE

IMPORTANT DOCUMENTS

WHAT	WHERE TO FIND IT	NOTE

NOTES

NOTES

FINANCES

MY ESTATE CUSTODIANS

THE EXECUTOR OF MY ESTATE IS	
CONTACT	THE SIGNED ORDER CAN BE FOUND

I HAVE NOMINATED THIS PERSON TO HOLD POWER OF ATTORNEY	
CONTACT	THE SIGNED ORDER CAN BE FOUND

SPECIAL NOTES TO MY ESTATE CUSTODIANS

 # BANK ACCOUNTS

TYPE	INSTITUTION	ACCOUNT NUMBER	CONTACT	NOTES
CREDIT CARD				
CHECKING ACC				
SAVINGS ACC				
DEBIT CARD				
PENSION FUND				

FIXED ASSETS

WHAT	WHERE TO FIND THE PAPERWORK	CONTACT	NOTES

FIXED ASSETS

WHAT	WHERE TO FIND THE PAPERWORK	CONTACT	NOTES

INVESTMENTS

WHAT	WHERE TO FIND THE PAPERWORK	CONTACT	NOTES

INVESTMENTS

WHAT	WHERE TO FIND THE PAPERWORK	CONTACT	NOTES

INCOME

WHO	WHAT FOR	AMOUNT	CONTACT	NOTES
	PENSION			
	GRANTS			
	PROPERTY RENTAL			
	SALARY			

 # MONEY I AM OWED

WHO	WHAT FOR	AMOUNT	CONTACT	NOTES

MONEY I AM OWED

WHO	WHAT FOR	AMOUNT	CONTACT	NOTES

DEBT & LIABILITIES

WHAT	WHERE TO FIND THE PAPERWORK	CONTACT	NOTES
MORTGAGE			
VEHICLE LOAN			
CREDIT CARD			
RETAIL ACCOUNT 1:			
RETAIL ACCOUNT 2:			

BILLS

WHO	WHAT FOR	APPROX. AMOUNT	CONTACT	NOTES
	MORTGAGE			
	VEHICLE			
	SCHOOL FEES			
	LOAN			
	UTILITIES			
	INTERNET			
	MOBILE CONTRACT			

NOTES

NOTES

LOOSE ENDS

WHERE TO FIND MY…

WHAT	WHERE	NOTES
ADDRESS BOOK		
HOUSE KEYS		
CAR KEYS		
SAFE KEY		
SAFETY DEPOSIT KEY		
IMPORTANT DOCUMENTS	*(SEE DOCUMENTS)*	
SAFE		
JEWELRY		
HEIRLOOMS		
COLLECTABLES		

SERVICES TO CLOSE AND CANCEL

SERVICE	ACCOUNT #	CONTACT	WEBSITE	ACCESS INFO
P.O. BOX				
MOBILE				
UTILITIES				
MAGAZINE				
NEWSPAPER				
CLEANERS				
GROOMERS				
GARDEN SERVICE				
GYM MEMBERSHIP				
TELEVISION				

SERVICES TO CLOSE AND CANCEL

SERVICE	ACCOUNT #	CONTACT	WEBSITE	ACCESS INFO

SPECIAL REQUESTS FOR MY BELONGINGS

SPECIAL REQUESTS FOR MY BELONGINGS

NOTES

NOTES

FINAL THOUGHTS

THESE PEOPLE KNOW ABOUT THIS JOURNAL

A NOTE TO THE BENEFICIARIES LISTED IN MY WILL

A NOTE TO THE PEOPLE I LOVE

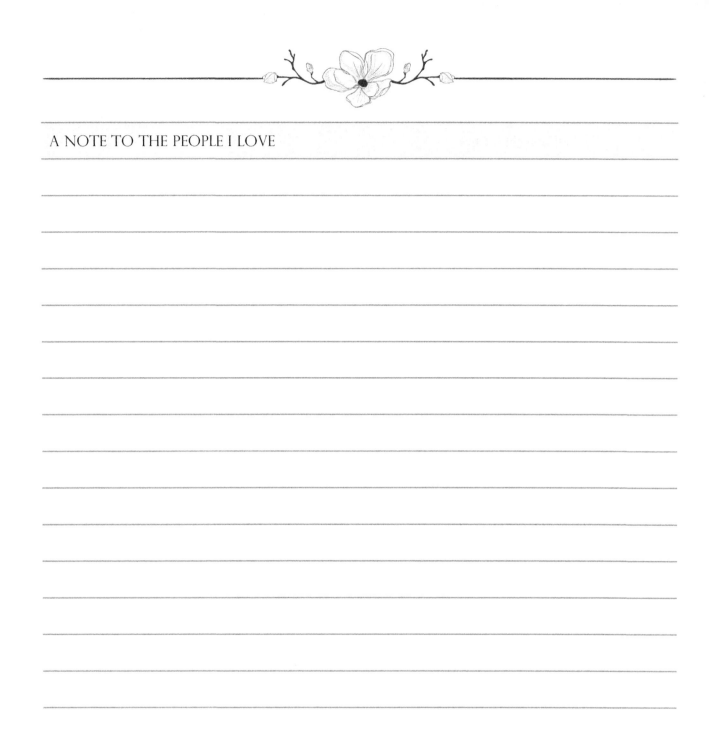

A NOTE TO THE PEOPLE I LOVE

MY FINAL WISHES

MY FINAL WISHES

MY FINAL WISHES

MY FINAL WISHES

NOTES

NOTES

NOTES

NOTES

NOTES

NOTES

NOTES

NOTES

NOTES

NOTES

NOTES

NOTES

NOTES

NOTES

NOTES

NOTES

NOTES

NOTES

NOTES

NOTES

 NOTES

NOTES

 # NOTES

NOTES

NOTES

NOTES

NOTES

NOTES

NOTES

NOTES

NOTES

NOTES

Made in the USA
Las Vegas, NV
25 August 2024